GREAT MARQUES POSTER BOOK

FERRARI

CHRIS HARVEY

OCTOPUS BOOKS

Contents

First published in 1986 by Octopus Books Limited, 59 Grosvenor Street, London W1

© 1986 Octopus Books Limited

ISBN 0 7064 2502 2

Produced by Mandarin Publishers Limited, 22a Westlands Road, Quarry Bay, Hong Kong

Printed in Hong Kong

Acknowledgements
Cars provided by Peter Agg/Trojan Ltd. (pages 5, 11), Donington Collection (7), M. Spitzley (9), the Harrisons (13), Ian Hilton (15), Vic Norman (17), Don Nelson (19), John Godfrey (21), Malcolm Clarke (23), Mark Tippetts (25), Ken Bradshaw (27), James Allington (29), D. Mason-Styrron (31), Kay Stubberfield (33), Robert Horne (35), The Patrick Collection (39), J. L. Barder (41), L. Page (43), Rob Abrahams (45)

Special photography:
LAT Photographic (pages 3, 37), Nicky Wright (5, 9–35, 43, 45), Ian Dawson (7, 39), Laurie J. Caddell (41), Neill Bruce Photographic (1, 47)

Page 1 Ferrari's 1984 Testa Rossa show car
Page 3 Michele Alboreto in action for Ferrari in the 1985 Portuguese Grand Prix

Introduction

No car could be more Italian than a Ferrari. That is because every one ever made was essentially the creation of one man, Enzo Ferrari, long venerated as Italy's greatest racing hero. Even now, when Ferraris are produced under the wing of the great Fiat empire, there are no committees at Maranello, near Modena. It is Enzo Ferrari himself who dictates the character of each of his cars, even if he leaves the design details to others. And Enzo, born in Modena on 18 February 1898, has always considered the engine to be the most important part of the car: its heart and its soul. Ferraris have always had marvellous engines; other aspects have to take second place to a searing exhaust note!

Enzo Ferrari went on record as saying that no real Ferrari could ever have less than 12 cylinders. Then, with a magnificent display of contradiction, he produced some of the best ever seen with eight, six, or only four. At one point he even denied the sixes (and one eight) the right to wear a Ferrari badge and named them Dinos, ostensibly in memory of his son.

Why did Ferrari start making cars under his own name in 1946 with 12-cylinder engines when practically everybody else made do with no more than eight? Because he was full of admiration for two splendid American engines, a V12 built by Packard before World War 2 when he was racing Alfa Romeos, and another made by Lincoln between 1932 and 1948. 'My cars will be inferior to none,' he said. 'They will have at least 12 cylinders.' He even experimented with 18!

Having put together the bones of his car, Ferrari then hired Gioacchino Colombo to design a new V12. This lovely little 1.5-litre unit had to be very strong and reliable because it was to be highly supercharged for grand prix racing, and available at the same time for use in sports cars in detuned form. Colombo's design has stood the test of time magnificently, forming the basis of 12-cylinder Ferraris right into the 1980s. The relationship between Ferrari the creator and Colombo the designer proved less durable. Colombo left to work for early rivals Maserati after his junior, Aurelio Lampredi, who had quit to join Isotta Fraschini, was lured back to Ferrari! When Lampredi returned in 1950, his brief was to design a four-cylinder grand prix unit which would use less fuel than the thirsty supercharged V12 – and so save pit stops – and at the same time produce a larger capacity unblown V12. Lampredi obliged and his bulky 'big block' V12 has formed the basis of all other Ferrari 12-cylinder engines.

There were occasions, however, when experiment indicated that other configurations might be better, so there was the odd in-line six-cylinder, and eventually a whole new family of V6s and a V8 based on portions of a V12. Subsequently, for reasons such as space, weight distribution and aerodynamics, a Colombo V12 was flattened into 'boxer' formation.

So much for the Ferrari engines, all of them interrelated. Until recent times, Ferrari chassis have tended to be basic, almost always built from a multitude of tubes. At first this was an advanced method of construction; though later, after gifted designers like Colin Chapman of Lotus had demonstrated that an ultra-lightweight monocoque was stronger, Ferrari still clung to what he knew best. In the same way, Ferrari's engines stayed in the front until British Coopers showed on the track that it was better to have the power unit behind the driver; eventually Lamborghini forced Ferrari to follow suit with his road cars. Ferrari also stuck to drum brakes for years after Jaguar had proved that discs were better, saying only 'A Ferrari is for go, not for stop!' In reality, he simply refused to be sidetracked by a new development until it had conclusively demonstrated its superiority and reliability. That Ferraris are unreliable is a myth, although some stay the pace better than others. They are invariably very strong, needing only skilled maintenance to outrun almost any other car.

Ferraris can be seen as racing cars for the road – or just as racing cars, for Ferrari has never been absent from the grand prix scene since 1946. Indeed, the early Ferraris were all racing cars, even if some of them were thinly disguised for road use. From 1953, however, they started to become what we know today: GP cars; sports racers; luxurious, limousine-like grand tourers; and very rapid two-seaters. At heart they are all the same: a wonderful howling engine clad in ever more sophisticated running gear.

Ferrari 195S

Ferrari 195S

It is ironic that, although Enzo Ferrari showed little interest in making road cars before 1955, those that were built have become enduring classics. They were almost invariably based on the 166 family of chassis, varying from thinly disguised grand prix cars to spartan grand tourers and only slightly more luxurious convertibles. The 166 designation was taken from the cubic capacity of one cylinder of the first, 2-litre, models. Developments on this theme with bored-out versions of the original Colombo V12 took the names 195 or 212 according to capacity. Hardly any two of the 250 or so cars made in these series were exactly alike. The 195, for instance, came in two versions: the Inter, with a single Weber twin-choke carburettor producing 130 bhp, and the Sport, or 195S, with triple Webers and a higher compression ratio, giving 145 bhp. The Inter was intended as a road touring car; the Sport was meant chiefly for competition and ran in the Mille Miglia and at Le Mans – unfortunately with little success.

All these cars were distinguished by a five-speed gearbox with synchromesh, initially, on third and fourth ratios only. First and second had to be straight cut for strength and fifth was intended only as an overdrive. Bodywork and wheelbase varied according to the customer's wishes: short-wheelbase cars were meant for competition, while the Inters generally had a longer wheelbase for comfort – although the specifications were juggled to produce all manner of variations. But all the cars of the 166 family had two-door bodies, in various two-seater styles: open sports, convertible or fixed-head coupé. In general, the open sports cars were intended for races such as the Mille Miglia, where visibility and light weight were of paramount importance; the fixed-head Sport coupés were meant mainly for events such as Le Mans, where driver fatigue and streamlining were important factors. The convertibles were better trimmed and aimed mainly at people who wanted a road car in a race style. All chassis were essentially the same, based on two massive steel tubes with cross members. Outwardly, however, the cars often looked totally different from each other, as all bodywork was built by specialists. Ferrari supplied only a rolling chassis. The best-remembered style of all was the classic coachwork by Carrozzeria Touring of Milan, as seen on the car illustrated.

ENGINE		CHASSIS	
Type	V	Frame	Tubular construction
No. of cylinders	12	Wheelbase mm	2500
Bore/stroke mm	65 x 58.8	Track – front mm	1270
Displacement cc	2341	Track – rear mm	1250
Valve operation	Single overhead camshaft	Suspension – front	Independent, wishbones and transverse leaf spring
Sparkplugs per cyl.	1		
Compression ratio	8.5:1	Suspension – rear	Live axle, half-elliptic springs
Induction	3 Weber carburettors		
BHP	145	Brakes	Drums front and rear
Transmission	Five-speed manual gearbox		
		PERFORMANCE	
		Maximum speed	209 km/h (130 mph)
		Fuel consumption	28.3 litres/100 km (10 mpg)

Ferrari 500

Ferrari 500

The big, brutal, four-cylinder Ferrari 500, first raced in 1951, became one of the world's most successful grand prix cars, winning 30 out of 33 consecutive races in three seasons. Ferrari had little effective opposition in those years, so everything about the 500 was aimed at reliability. Its chassis followed traditional lines for the marque, with two massive tubular side members braced by cross tubes. The suspension was rugged in the extreme, with two sturdy transverse leaf springs at its heart.

The engine, however, represented a departure from Ferrari's previous practice as it had only four cylinders. This was partly for reliability, because there were fewer working components to fail; partly to cut the earlier V12's fuel consumption; and partly to improve torque through a longer stroke. Reliability was the governing factor, reflected not only in the sheer size and strength of the car's main components, but in the thinking that lay behind reducing the fuel consumption. A less thirsty car faced fewer pit stops and could get away with carrying less fuel, and thus less weight, which improved its potential reliability. When combined with the better pulling power – or torque – from the four-cylinder engine, this reduction in overall weight meant that the car was faster away from corners. It thus spent more time travelling flat out than a car that had to haul along a lot of extra fuel for only a very slightly higher top speed, gained by extra power at the top end.

The retirement at the end of 1951 of the previously all-conquering supercharged Alfa Romeos (which used a lot of fuel) left Ferrari as the only real contender for the world championship, so the stage for this contest switched from Formula One to Formula Two, where some opposition remained.

Ferrari built its new GP car in two forms: as the 500 with a 2-litre version of the four-cylinder engine to comply with Formula Two regulations; and as the 625 with a bored-out 2.5-litre engine for such races as were run under this higher capacity limit (later to become Formula One in 1954). Hardly any other car could stay with the new Ferraris in either form; the works team leader Alberto Ascari duly took the world drivers' championship in 1952 and 1953, before the 500 and 625 were superseded.

ENGINE		CHASSIS	
Type	In-line	**Frame**	Tubular construction
No. of cylinders	4	**Wheelbase mm**	2160
Bore/stroke mm	90 x 78	**Track – front mm**	1270
Displacement cc	1985	**Track – rear mm**	1250
Valve operation	Twin overhead camshafts	**Suspension – front**	Independent, wishbone and transverse leaf spring
Sparkplugs per cyl.	2		
Compression ratio	12.8 : 1	**Suspension – rear**	de Dion, transverse leaf spring, trailing arms
Induction	Four Weber carburettors		
BHP	180	**Brakes**	Drums front and rear
Transmission	Four-speed manual gearbox		
		PERFORMANCE	
		Maximum speed	257 km/h (160 mph) average according to gearing
		Fuel consumption	23.5 litres/100 km (12 mpg) average

Ferrari 121LM

Ferrari 121LM

Throughout the 1950s, Ferrari constantly interchanged features of its grand prix and sports cars, trying out permutations and combinations that produced a bewildering array of vehicles. One line of development pursued was to bore out the four-cylinder GP engines to as much as 3 litres, and install them in a 166, or the later 250, sports car chassis. The first of these cars made its début at Monza in 1953 and subsequently bore the name of the Italian track.

The next experiments centred on adding two cylinders to the Monza's engine to see what happened! A similar addition to a 2.5-litre 625 engine in a model called the Mondial had led to a 3.7-litre sports racer called the 118LM (for Le Mans); the new, larger, car was then known as the 121LM, with a capacity of 4.4 litres. The basic idea was to produce a sports car that was rugged, to say the least, but not too thirsty: both were important considerations for long-distance racing. Unfortunately, these machines were among the wildest ever made and proved very difficult to handle.

The 121LM was certainly fast enough in a straight line to cope with the opposition, but was a handful in corners and on rough surfaces. The chief opposition came from Mercedes with the 300SLR, based on the W196 GP car, which gave a better ride than the Ferrari, but still had tricky handling; and Jaguar, with an aircraft-styled D type, which had far better disc brakes but only marginally better roadholding than the Italian car.

Ferrari's preoccupation with engine development had caused the company to neglect its chassis, with the result that the 121LM, in particular, had trouble conveying its considerable power to the ground. This did not present too much of a problem on a smooth circuit like Le Mans, but was a distinct handicap on the rough roads of the Mille Miglia. The 121LMs managed to stay ahead of the Jaguars and Mercedes at Le Mans in 1955 before they were eliminated with minor problems, ceding victory to Jaguar. They did the same in the Mille Miglia until excessive wheelspin burned up their tyres, while the same problem led to mechanical breakages on the 118LMs also entered by Ferrari for this race. The Mercedes, with their better ride, combined with the brilliant driving of Stirling Moss, romped home in the Italian event. The 121LMs and 118LMs should be remembered, with Maserati's ferocious 450S, as dinosaurs: the last of their coarse-grained breed of sports racing car.

ENGINE		CHASSIS	
Type	In-line	**Frame**	Tubular construction
No. of cylinders	6	**Wheelbase mm**	2400
Bore/stroke mm	102 x 90	**Track – front mm**	1278
Displacement cc	4413	**Track – rear mm**	1284
Valve operation	Twin overhead camshafts	**Suspension – front**	Independent, wishbones and coil springs
Sparkplugs per cyl.	2		
Compression ratio	8.5:1	**Suspension – rear**	de Dion, transverse leaf spring
Induction	3 Weber carburettors		
BHP	330	**Brakes**	Drums front and rear
Transmission	Five-speed manual transaxle		

PERFORMANCE	
Maximum speed	282 km/h (175 mph)
Fuel consumption	28.3 litres/100 km (10 mpg)

Ferrari Superfast

Ferrari Superfast

The first pure road cars built by Ferrari were intended for the North American market where there were enough wealthy customers to afford their very high prices. One of the reasons these cars were so expensive was that they were virtually all 'one-offs', featuring the most exotic coachwork. Most of them were very powerful, using the Lampredi-designed V12-cylinder engine, and all of them had the same, basic, tubular chassis as the sports racing cars, differing only in that they had a longer wheelbase.

The first of this series was the 342 America, built in 1953 and 1954 with a 4.1-litre single overhead camshaft engine that had been used in Ferrari's 1950 GP car, and in the 340 Mexico and MM sports cars of that period. It was substantially detuned, however, to make it more manageable on the road; and with a power output of only 220 bhp it was something of a flop on the American market.

Soon after, therefore, the engine was bored out to 4.5 litres with a higher state of tune taking it to 300 bhp. The 375 America, as this car was known, was bigger than the 342, but lighter, which meant that with the extra power it could then easily outrun the best

American V8s of the day. Its power still did not match that of the bigger Ferrari sports racers, however, so late in 1954 the engine was again uprated to 4.9 litres, in almost the same state of tune as the V12s which had won the Buenos Aires 1000-kilometre race, Le Mans and the Carrera Panamericana road race in Mexico. Ferrari's fabulously rich customers were demanding, and getting, a super luxury version of this top sports racing car, called – not surprisingly – the 410 Superamerica.

Although the 410 Superamerica was sufficiently exclusive for the needs of most wealthy clients, there were others who wanted something even more glamorous – and were willing to pay a fortune for it. This minute market, consisting chiefly of European royalty and industrial magnates, was catered for by a number of amazing variants on the big-engined theme. The first Ferrari of this type appeared in 1956 and was capable of 270 km/h (168 mph). It featured a full-race 4.9-litre engine in a shorter 250GT chassis with spectacular Pinin Farina cantilever-roofed bodywork in which the windscreen pillars were deleted. It was called the Superfast.

ENGINE		CHASSIS	
Type	V	**Frame**	Tubular construction
No. of cylinders	12	**Wheelbase mm**	2596
Bore/stroke mm	88 x 68	**Track – front mm**	1351
Displacement cc	4963	**Track – rear mm**	1346
Valve operation	Single overhead camshaft	**Suspension – front**	Independent, wishbones and coil springs
Sparkplugs per cyl.	1		
Compression ratio	8.5:1	**Suspension – rear**	Live axle and half-elliptic springs
Induction	3 Weber carburettors		
BHP	340	**Brakes**	Drums front and rear
Transmission	Four-speed manual gearbox		
		PERFORMANCE	
		Maximum speed	270 km/h (168 mph)
		Fuel consumption	23.94 litres/100 km (11.8 mpg)

Ferrari 250 Testa Rossa

Ferrari Testa Rossa

The name Testa Rossa ('red head') became one of the most emotive in Ferrari history when it was given to a series of sports racing cars distinguished by the red crackle finish on the cylinder heads of their engines. Red was traditionally used to denote the most powerful variant among a manufacturer's engines; in this case it was applied to what was being offered in sports cars rather than single-seaters. Although the name Testa Rossa has become universally associated with V12-cylinder cars, the first Testa Rossas had 2-litre four-cylinder engines, followed by 2.5-litre units based closely on the 625 grand prix motor. These Tipo 500 cars proved quite competitive in 1956 – one example taking third place at Le Mans – before they went into series production for customers as the factory concentrated on Tipo 250 Testa Rossas: powered by highly tuned versions of the Ferrari 250GT's V12 single overhead camshaft unit – again with a red head.

It was also during this period that the company finally started to update its suspension for general use, and de Dion rear axle assemblies took over in some cases from the old live rear axle. In general, factory-entered cars had the de Dion set-up while customer cars stuck to the tried and tested live axle. Engines also gradually changed from old-style hairpin valve springs to more modern coils. A similar change, from the old leaf springs to coils, was made in the suspension. There was also considerable experiment with the bodywork.

Testa Rossas built between late 1957 and mid-1958 had strange pontoon-style front wings: they represented an attempt to provide better cooling for the front brakes, and hence more speed, but this was negated, as it turned out, by the lift the wings generated. Most early Testa Rossas also had either wide cut-outs behind the wheels to let out hot air, or a variety of ducts. Later models received more conventional bodywork as Enzo Ferrari was at last persuaded to try the new-fangled disc brakes. No fewer than ten Testa Rossas were entered for Le Mans in 1958 and, sure enough, one of them won. This was followed by a third successive world sports car championship for the marque. After that Testa Rossas continued winning until 1962, with ever more advanced bodywork, and, eventually, independent rear suspension – but always with the same fiery red-headed engine.

ENGINE		CHASSIS	
Type	V	**Frame**	Tubular construction
No. of cylinders	12	**Wheelbase mm**	2350
Bore/stroke mm	73 x 58.8	**Track – front mm**	1308
Displacement cc	2953	**Track – rear mm**	1300
Valve operation	Single overhead camshaft	**Suspension – front**	Independent, wishbone and coil springs
Sparkplugs per cyl.	1		
Compression ratio	9.8:1	**Suspension – rear**	Live axle, half-elliptic springs, trailing arms
Induction	Six Weber carburettors	**Brakes**	Drums front and rear
BHP	300		
Transmission	Four-speed manual gearbox	**PERFORMANCE**	
		Maximum speed	266 km/h (165 mph)
		Fuel consumption	28.3 litres/100 km (10 mpg)

Ferrari 250GTS California

250GTS California

A 3-litre version of the 342 and 375 Ferrari road cars was built from 1953 for customers in Europe who were hard hit by taxation based on engine capacity. This car, the 250 Europa, finally convinced Enzo Ferrari that decent profits could be made from series production machines, and it evolved into the 250GT for 1955.

The first thing that was changed was the engine, from a scaled-down version of the Lampredi-designed 'big block' V12 to the outwardly smaller, but still 3-litre, Colombo V12, which had the benefit of being more reliable. The same type of tubular chassis that had been used on the Europa was retained, but with a shorter wheelbase to make a much more sporting two-seater. Coil spring suspension also became standard for the first time on a road-going Ferrari. The Europa's four-speed gearbox and spiral bevel drive rear axle were not changed, however, as they had proved thoroughly reliable in service.

Ferrari did not make its own bodies, and with the exception of special versions, most of the 250GT's coachwork was styled by Pinin Farina (Pininfarina after 1958) and more often than not built by

Scaglietti near the works in Modena. Although most 250GTs had the fixed-head bodywork normally associated with a grand touring car, some convertibles were built and sold chiefly on the west coast of America, where good weather could be guaranteed. These cars soon became known as Californias, with the common suffix of S-for-spyder added to their basic 250GT designation.

Spyder was the name given by Italians to a light racing carriage of skimpy design that seemed to scuttle along behind its horse, moving much as a spider does. The name was then given by extension to sports cars with minimal competition bodywork: the heirs apparent to the trotting horse buggies remembered with such affection in Italy.

Subsequently the name spyder was transferred to open convertibles, so that drivers could impress their friends by proclaiming their ownership of a real racing car. There was nothing skimpy about the construction of the California, though, and these cars were frequently adorned with heavy chrome fittings to attract American customers.

ENGINE		CHASSIS	
Type	V	Frame	Tubular construction
No. of cylinders	12	Wheelbase mm	2596
Bore/stroke mm	73 x 58.8	Track – front mm	1351
Displacement cc	2953	Track – rear mm	1346
Valve operation	Single overhead camshaft	Suspension – front	Independent, wishbones and coil springs
Sparkplugs per cyl.	1		
Compression ratio	8.5 : 1	Suspension – rear	Live axle, half-elliptic springs
Induction	3 Weber carburettors		
BHP	240	Brakes	Drums front and rear
Transmission	Four-speed manual gearbox		
		PERFORMANCE	
		Maximum speed	219 km/h (136 mph)
		Fuel consumption	20.2 litres/100 km (14 mpg)

Ferrari 250GT

Ferrari 250GT

By 1955 sports racing cars such as the Ferrari 121LM and Mercedes 300SLR had become as fast as GP machines while frequently falling into amateur hands. It needed only the appalling Le Mans accident of that year, in which 82 people were killed when a disintegrating Mercedes flew into the crowd, to start a movement back to the classic conception of sports racing cars more closely aligned to road machines.

Ferrari was well placed in this context, having just put the 250GT into production. As luxurious versions were built for some customers, other cars were produced to a similar mechanical specification, but with far lighter bodywork which just complied with new GT racing regulations. These berlinettas – or 'little saloons' – became immediately popular in events such as the Tour de France, a series of circuit races and hill-climbs round France, linked by long road sections.

Few other GT cars could stay with these Ferraris on the road. This delighted numerous wealthy amateur drivers who could now contest GT classes in the classic road races. Soon the bodywork became lighter and lighter, and it was obvious that any further improvements would have to come from the chassis for the GT racing regulations governed mechanical specifications quite closely, refusing to allow one-off cars like the Testa Rossas.

In 1959, the 250GT chassis was shortened still further from the original Europa's specification, with the lightest possible bodywork, to form the classic short-wheelbase berlinetta. Disc brakes were also fitted to make these cars even more formidable in GT racing. The great disadvantage of the ultra-lightweight aluminium bodywork, however, was that it was very easily damaged; if anybody sat on a wing, for instance, it was likely to be severely dented! So, for general use, the bodies were produced in steel but with lightweight styling for customers who wanted their car to look like a racer without sharing its impracticalities.

This form of production was also of great help to Ferrari in its attempts to qualify the short-wheelbase berlinetta for GT racing, where the regulations decreed that more than 100 almost identical cars had to have been built.

ENGINE		CHASSIS	
Type	V	Frame	Tubular construction
No. of cylinders	12	Wheelbase mm	2596
Bore/stroke mm	73 x 58.8	Track – front mm	1351
Displacement cc	2953	Track – rear mm	1346
Valve operation	Single overhead camshaft	Suspension – front	Independent, wishbones and coil springs
Sparkplugs per cyl.	1		
Compression ratio	8.5 : 1	Suspension – rear	Live axle, half-elliptic springs
Induction	3 Weber carburettors		
BHP	240	Brakes	Discs front and rear
Transmission	Four-speed manual gearbox		
		PERFORMANCE	
		Maximum speed	219 km/h (136 mph)
		Fuel consumption	20.2 litres/100 km (14 mpg)

Ferrari 250GTO

Ferrari 250GTO

Ferrari was winning so many races in the world sports car championship that no other marque stood a realistic chance of taking the title in the early 1960s. So the controlling body, the FIA (Fédération Internationale de l'Automobile) decided to change the rules in the hope that it would give somebody else a chance and thus keep the interest of the crowds.

The FIA decided that the 1962 world championship series would be contested only by GT cars of 3 litres maximum capacity. Some race organizers, such as those at Le Mans, refused to go along with this edict, fearing that their events would lose much of their crowd-pulling spectacle. They insisted, therefore, on retaining a special prototype category.

This sort of situation suited Enzo Ferrari very well. He could build cars to fit into any category from his extraordinary portfolio of engines, chassis and bodies! He realized, however, that the 250GT berlinettas needed more speed if they were to win the world title against the fierce opposition provided by cars such as lightweight versions of the Jaguar E type – based on the earlier D type – and the Aston Martin DB4GT Zagato.

Experiments to improve the aerodynamics of the Testa Rossa had been quite successful, and its engine was absolutely dependable, so Ferrari decided to combine the best of both cars. The chassis of the 250GT had to remain essentially the same, otherwise not even Ferrari could claim that more than 100 had been made. But he gave it the latest Testa Rossa engine in its low-line dry-sump form and a body remodelled along the lines of the 410 Superamerica, which had a very low nose for better air penetration. Experiments with spoilers on the tails of Testa Rossas had worked well, too, so the new Ferrari GT cars acquired those as well.

Ferrari's rivals complained bitterly that the new car was so far removed from a normal 250GT that it should not qualify for GT racing. Ferrari even admitted that he had no intention of building 100 of them, but the FIA still declared the car legal for fear of losing a great crowd-puller. This strange qualifying process was known as homologation (*omologato* in Italian) so the new car became the 250GTO. Suffice it to say that it won the world title for three successive years.

ENGINE		CHASSIS	
Type	V	**Frame**	Tubular construction
No. of cylinders	12	**Wheelbase mm**	2596
Bore/stroke mm	73 x 58.8	**Track – front mm**	1351
Displacement cc	2953	**Track – rear mm**	1346
Valve operation	Single overhead camshaft	**Suspension – front**	Independent, wishbones and coil springs
Sparkplugs per cyl.	1		
Compression ratio	9.8 : 1	**Suspension – rear**	Live axle, half-elliptic springs
Induction	6 Weber carburettors		
BHP	300	**Brakes**	Drums front and rear
Transmission	Five-speed manual gearbox		
		PERFORMANCE	
		Maximum speed	283 km/h (176 mph)
		Fuel consumption	28.3 litres/100 km (10 mpg)

Ferrari 196SP

Ferrari 196SP

The reason Enzo Ferrari insisted on calling some of his cars Dinos remains shadowy. He cites the influence of his son in his memoirs, but he has also given credit in this matter to his designer, Vittorio Jano. No matter what the true reason, there were three distinct series of V6 Dino engines and one V8 (dispelling notions that all Dinos were V6 cars). The first series began with Formula Two engines which had twin overhead camshafts, twin ignition systems, dry-sump lubrication, and capacities varying between 1.5 and 3 litres. Their engine layout was unusual, with the banks of cylinders opposed at 65 degrees to make room for their inlet manifolding. These were complex engines and were featured only in works machines.

A later series of V6s was built along simpler lines, which amounted to half a 250GT (or Testa Rossa) engine, its narrower single overhead camshaft cylinder heads allowing the use of the better balanced 60-degree formation. Single ignition was also featured, the idea being to keep down the cost of customer cars. Later still, when there were hopes of selling a number of these racing cars, two were built with 90-degree V8s – virtually two-thirds of a 400 Superamerica engine – but still called Dinos! Ferrari then went on to develop a later 65-degree V6 Dino engine for use in a Fiat sports car so that the power unit could be homologated for a new Formula Two.

Dino racing cars were built in numerous forms, initially as single-seaters with the first 65-degree engine, and then from 1957 as sports racing cars of smaller capacity than the Testa Rossas. These performed reasonably well and their 65-degree engines were enlarged to 3 litres for comparison with the V12 units.

The 60-degree V6 was developed in 1958 for a Dino designated 196S: all Dinos had been given a new numbering system in which the first two figures denoted the capacity (19 for 1.9 litres), and the third the number of cylinders (6 for a V6), with the addition of (for instance) an S for Sports or SP for Sports Prototype. At first these Dinos suffered from a lack of development, but subsequently they managed to counter the growing menace of Porsche's new sports racing cars. The mid-engined 196SP introduced in 1962 featured a distinctive Carlo Chiti-designed shark's nose, intended for better air penetration; the GT equivalent, the 250GTO, kept a normal oval shape, however, so that it avoided looking too much like a sports racing car!

ENGINE		CHASSIS	
Type	V	Frame	Tubular construction
No. of cylinders	6	Wheelbase mm	2320
Bore/stroke mm	77 x 71	Track – front mm	1310
Displacement cc	1983	Track – rear mm	1300
Valve operation	Single overhead camshaft	Suspension – front	Independent, wishbones and coil springs
Sparkplugs per cyl.	1		
Compression ratio	9.8:1	Suspension – rear	Independent, wishbones and coil springs
Induction	3 Weber carburettors		
BHP	210		
Transmission	Five-speed manual gearbox	Brakes	Discs front and rear

PERFORMANCE	
Maximum speed	225 km/h (140 mph)
Fuel consumption	28.3 litres/100 km (10 mpg)

Ferrari 250GT Lusso

Ferrari 250GT Lusso

The 250GTO's body was never produced in steel for normal road-going use because the special low-drag nose was impractical. It featured three flaps which could be opened by hand when the car was stationary for those rare occasions when it might be driven slowly. Its cooling normally relied upon a constant blast of fresh air – which could only be generated at high speed – through the small, fixed air intake. But with the 250GTO's success in competition, there naturally followed a demand for a more luxurious road-going version and Ferrari filled this gap amply with the 250GT Lusso berlinetta introduced late in 1962.

Like the GTO, this car was to become one of the most revered Ferraris: its lovely lines, designed by Pininfarina, took much of their inspiration from the racing machine. The nose of the earlier short-wheelbase 250GT berlinettas had to be retained for practical reasons, but the tail had a vestige of the GTO's spoiler, neatly faired in rather than just riveted on as with the early racing cars. The new Lusso also had small bumpers front and rear and the same size wheels all round, for practical reasons; this meant that it did not need the GTO's hunched rear wheel arches to clear oversize tyres. Many people, therefore, considered the Lusso ('luxury') to be the better-looking car. There was also more light inside following the addition of glass rear side windows (heavier than aluminium panels) and the interior was much more comfortable.

The chassis was basically the same as that of the GTO – and all the 250GTs before it – but the engine was detuned to 250 bhp to make it more appropriate for road use. The Lusso also managed to do without the cooling slots cut in the front wings, so badly needed by the GTO.

In an attempt to publicize the new car, and to justify the homologation of the 250GTO, one 250GTO was raced at Le Mans in 1963 with a roof and rear windows that followed the style of the Lusso. The Lusso continued in production throughout 1964 as the 250GTO was rebodied to look as much as possible like Ferrari's later mid-engined sports racer, the 250P: this was an attempt to have the even more limited production 250LM homologated as a replacement for the 250GTO. Only about 40 GTOs were built, whereas Ferrari's production of road cars like the Lusso rose to hundreds in this period, such was their popularity.

ENGINE		CHASSIS	
Type	V	Frame	Tubular construction
No. of cylinders	12	Wheelbase mm	2596
Bore/stroke mm	73 x 58.8	Track – front mm	1351
Displacement cc	2953	Track – rear mm	1346
Valve operation	Single overhead camshaft	Suspension – front	Independent, wishbones and coil springs
Sparkplugs per cyl.	1		
Compression ratio	8.5:1	Suspension – rear	Live axle, half-elliptic springs
Induction	3 Weber carburettors		
BHP	250	Brakes	Drums front and rear
Transmission	Four-speed manual gearbox		
		PERFORMANCE	
		Maximum speed	241 km/h (150 mph)
		Fuel consumption	20.2 litres/100 km (14 mpg)

Ferrari 250LM

Ferrari 250LM

Ferrari only really began to follow the modern mid-engined trend, pioneered by Cooper and Porsche, with the Dino 246SP in 1961, when it was obvious that front-engined racing cars had been rendered obsolete. His next step was logical: a Testa Rossa engine was installed in a slightly longer Dino chassis towards the end of 1962 and it confirmed its potential by breaking the Monza lap record in testing. Ferrari was upset, however, when people pointed to the new 250P's shark nose and said that Carlo Chiti's influence lived on: his chief engineer had left earlier in the year to join Alfa Romeo. So the 250P was given a more conventional front for the 1963 season. Following a successful year, a closed version of the 250P called the LM (for Le Mans) was introduced for 1964 – and Enzo Ferrari requested that it should be homologated for GT racing in place of the GTO!

Apart from sharing the same engine and front suspension as the already marginally qualified GTO, the 250LM was a completely different car (though the GTO had been rebodied in similar form). The 250LM had a tubular spaceframe and independent rear suspension like the Dino and, at that time, only one had been produced. The FIA refused point-blank to homologate it as a series production grand tourer of which more than 100 had been built: the Federation's hand had been strengthened in this case by the arrival of an American team of AC Cobras to keep the crowds' interest in GT racing lively.

Ferrari did not give up hope of getting the 250LM homologated, however, once he had built a few more. These were, in reality, pure racing cars – rather than GT cars which could be sold off for road use – so they were given more power to make them competitive in prototype classes. The faithful V12 engine was bored out to 3.3 litres but the designation was not changed to the logical 275LM because Ferrari was still claiming that it was, after all, a member of the 250GT family!

The 250LMs raced sporadically throughout 1964 as the rebodied 250GTOs won their world championship again; the FIA still refused to homologate the 250LM for 1965 as only about 20 had been built – with 3.3-litre engines. It was not until Ferrari had uprated the 250GT range to 275 specification that the 250LM was finally homologated in 1966. Private entrants had become more successful by then, however, finishing first and second at Le Mans in 1965 as faster prototypes failed.

ENGINE		CHASSIS	
Type	V	Frame	Tubular construction
No. of cylinders	12	Wheelbase mm	2400
Bore/stroke mm	77 x 58.8	Track – front mm	1352
Displacement cc	3286	Track – rear mm	1340
Valve operation	Single overhead camshaft	Suspension – front	Independent, wishbones and coil springs
Sparkplugs per cyl.	1		
Compression ratio	9.8:1	Suspension – rear	Independent, wishbones and coil springs
Induction	6 Weber carburettors		
BHP	330	Brakes	Discs front and rear
Transmission	Five-speed manual gearbox		
		PERFORMANCE	
		Maximum speed	290 km/h (180 mph)
		Fuel consumption	28.3 litres/100 km (10 mpg)

Ferrari 500 Superfast

Ferrari 500 Superfast

The first Ferrari Superfast show car, known retrospectively as the Superfast I, proved very influential. Many of its styling features, including its long, elliptical grilled nose, were used on later Ferraris. Pinin Farina reproduced this car in essence in 1957 but without the special roof and fins, which were becoming rather dated. This car was called the Ferrari 4.9 Superfast.

Later versions of the basic 410 Superamerica followed this styling until the heavy Lampredi engine was phased out in 1960 to be replaced by a 4-litre version of the Colombo V12 for a model called the 400 Superamerica – causing some confusion as it was a first deviation from Ferrari's normal numbering policy. It was also given a different chassis, that of the 250GT cars which had been used in the Superfast models. Soon after, a longer-wheelbase variant of this chassis was developed for a two-plus-two seater version of the 250GT, called the 250GTE, and the 400 Superamerica naturally offered it as an option.

But there was still the odd 410 Superamerica chassis lying around unused, and one was shortened to be fitted with special coachwork for Pininfarina's personal use in 1961. His car was then called the Superfast II! Again its styling formed a theme for the 400SAs to follow, some of which were spyders and some berlinettas. A second Superfast II was then constructed on the short-wheelbase 400SA chassis which was to be exhibited later in 1961.

This car was superseded the following year by a Superfast III; it had new styling, but continued the theme of an especially light and airy cabin. The cantilever roof was abandoned, but the glass-to-glass seal reappeared in place of the middle roof pillars this time! This model retained the retractable headlamps of the Superfast II cars, but incorporated a similar retractable radiator grille cover as well. A fourth Superfast then appeared with a twin-headlight system that was to be featured on a new larger-engined 250GTE, called the 330GT.

The 400SA was replaced in 1964 by a 500 Superfast that was to go into normal production. This had a 4.9-litre engine producing 400 bhp, but based on the Colombo design. The chassis was similar to the 330GT, but the coachwork was as exclusive as it had ever been on the Superamericas.

ENGINE		CHASSIS	
Type	V	**Frame**	Tubular construction
No. of cylinders	12	**Wheelbase mm**	2598
Bore/stroke mm	88 x 68	**Track – front mm**	1483
Displacement cc	4962	**Track – rear mm**	1478
Valve operation	Single overhead camshaft	**Suspension – front**	Independent, wishbones and coil springs
Sparkplugs per cyl.	1		
Compression ratio	8.8 : 1	**Suspension – rear**	Live axle and half-elliptic springs
Induction	3 Weber carburettors		
BHP	400	**Brakes**	Discs front and rear
Transmission	Five-speed manual gearbox		
		PERFORMANCE	
		Maximum speed	266 km/h (165 mph)
		Fuel consumption	24 litres/100 km (11.8 mpg)

Ferrari 275GTB/4

Ferrari 275GTB/4

The Ferrari 275GTB (for berlinetta) or 275GTS (for spyder), introduced late in 1964 to replace the Lusso, can be viewed as the first of the modern Ferrari grand touring cars, although it retained the classic front-engined configuration. This is because it was the first Ferrari GT car to use independent rear suspension, which had been developed on earlier single-seaters and prototype sports racing cars as well as the 250LM. The engine, produced at first in triple-carburettor form, produced 260 bhp from the same capacity as the 3.3-litre 250LM; and a more powerful version, with six carburettors and a higher compression ratio, was offered as an option for a 300 bhp competition car called the 275GTB/C.

These 275GT cars handled far better than the earlier 250s, not only because of their new rear suspension, but because they were equipped with a five-speed all-synchromesh transaxle, which improved their weight distribution. This was initially linked to the normal clutch and engine by an open propeller shaft, which unfortunately vibrated in normal use and gave trouble unless it was very accurately set up and constantly maintained. The bodywork followed the general lines of the earlier GTOs (rather than the rebodied 1964 examples) and was offered in steel or aluminium.

Then, in 1966, this rapid machine was further improved with six carburettors as standard, and a longer nose for better air penetration. Normal production models were also fitted with magnesium wheels and a torque tube to eliminate the transmission troubles. Competition versions, however, were made only with aluminium bodies, and kept the earlier open shaft to make transmission work easier during pit stops. They also kept the earlier quick-change wire wheels.

However, the most significant change to all models came late in 1966 when they received twin-camshaft cylinder heads and a dry-sump lubrication as the 275GTB/4 family. This allowed the use of the higher power output without resorting to a very high compression ratio. During 1967 a few 3-litre competition versions were made, called the 250GTB/4C, and there was a short run of 275GTB/4s in open form for North American competition with 3.3-litre 250LM engines and spartan trim. The rest of the line continued in 275GTB/4 fixed-head coupé or 275GTS/4 open form with either aluminium or steel bodies.

ENGINE		CHASSIS	
Type	V	Frame	Tubular construction
No. of cylinders	12	Wheelbase mm	2398
Bore/stroke mm	77 x 58.8	Track – front mm	1403
Displacement cc	3286	Track – rear mm	1417
Valve operation	Twin overhead camshafts	Suspension – front	Independent, wishbones and coil springs
Sparkplugs per cyl.	1		
Compression ratio	9.2 : 1	Suspension – rear	Independent, wishbones and coil springs
Induction	6 Weber carburettors		
BHP	300		
Transmission	Five-speed manual transaxle	Brakes	Discs front and rear
		PERFORMANCE	
		Maximum speed	268 km/h (166 mph)
		Fuel consumption	19 litres/100 km (14.9 mpg)

Ferrari 206S

Ferrari 206S

The Ferrari Dino 206S represents one strand of an ill-fated plan by Enzo Ferrari and Fiat to establish a new marque called Dino whereby Fiat would produce relatively large quantities of Ferrari-inspired sports cars to the ultimate benefit of both parties. The first such car to emerge from Modena to publicize this bond, carrying 'Dino' on its bonnet instead of the Prancing Horse of Ferrari, was the 166P coupé which made its début at Monza in 1965. In appearance, it was a scaled-down version of the 4-litre 330P2 sports racing car that Ferrari was fielding as a front runner in endurance events; in reality it was a sports racing variant of a highly successful V6 1.5-litre Ferrari Formula One car.

As such it was powered by a 1600 cc grand prix-style engine, with dual ignition twin overhead camshaft cylinder heads necessitating a 65-degree angle between the cylinder banks. The idea was that this should be a prototype for a Ferrari production sports racing car, the engine of which would be built in sufficient numbers for a road car by Fiat so that it could be homologated for Formula Two racing. At first this Dino was quite successful, running as high as third overall in the Nürburgring 1000 Kilometres before finishing a spectacular, misfiring, fourth. In fact the Ferrari team had to strip the engine after the event to prove that it was of only 1600 cc!

For much of the rest of the 1965 season, Ferrari Dinos in open and closed forms were driven by Lodovico Scarfiotti in the European Mountain championship where their chief competitors, the Porsches, were particularly strong. Scarfiotti, however, was so successful with a 2-litre Dino spyder, the 206SP, that he managed to take the title.

By 1966 it was hoped that at least 50 of these Dinos would be built to qualify them as production sports racing cars. With this object in mind, the 206SP was then revised as the 206S, with a more basic single-ignition engine which had a lower compression ratio for better reliability. At the same time, it had benefited from development on the previous season's GP cars. But labour unrest at Modena severely disrupted Ferrari's racing and development work, and it was not possible to build enough Dino 206S cars. As a result, works examples were fitted with more powerful dual ignition, fuel injection engines, and one spyder came within an ace of achieving victory in the Nürburgring 1000 Kilometres event in 1966.

ENGINE		CHASSIS	
Type	V	**Frame**	Tubular construction
No. of cylinders	6	**Wheelbase mm**	2330
Bore/stroke mm	86 x 57	**Track – front mm**	1232
Displacement cc	1987	**Track – rear mm**	1200
Valve operation	Twin overhead camshafts	**Suspension – front**	Independent, wishbones and coil springs
Sparkplugs per cyl.	2		
Compression ratio	10.8:1	**Suspension – rear**	Independent, wishbones and coil springs
Induction	Lucas fuel injection		
BHP	230		
Transmission	Five-speed manual transaxle	**Brakes**	Discs front and rear
		PERFORMANCE	
		Maximum speed	283 km/h (176 mph)
		Fuel consumption	28.3 litres/100 km (10 mpg)

Ferrari 206GT

Ferrari 206GT

Such was the enduring beauty of the Dino 206s that it would have been a tragedy not to have put them into production – a view reinforced by the profits made by Porsche from its 911, which had taken advantage of the German marque's reputation in endurance racing. Fiat, meanwhile, was anxious to go ahead with its own front-engined sports car powered by a 'Ferrari engine'. As a result, Fiat started to build the 206S unit in 1967 in detuned form for its own car, and provided enough engines for Ferrari to build a GT car and use the cylinder block for its Formula Two effort.

At this point, the intention was for the front-engined Dino (by Fiat) to sell as a medium-priced sports car in a market dominated by the Jaguar E type, while the mid-engined Dino (by Ferrari) took sales from Porsche, at that time dominating the more expensive GT field with the 911. Pininfarina styled both Dinos along the lines of the 206S, the new Ferrari being called the 206GT. Fiat built its Dino on its own production lines at first and Scaglietti began to build the aluminium bodies for the Dino 206GT. But both cars proved to be more expensive to produce than expected; the

206GT in particular was elevated to a price realm formerly occupied by Ferrari's front-engined GT cars. At that point, all pretence was dropped that it was anything other than a Ferrari!

The main market for such cars was, as always, the United States, which was imposing ever more stringent exhaust emission regulations. These sapped an engine's power, so the obvious way to maintain the performance so vital to such models was to increase the capacity of the engine. Introducing a higher degree of tune, nearer to that used in the 206S, almost invariably meant that the engine ran hotter, a problem that was already causing concern in California, the biggest individual market in America.

The Dino was therefore increased to 2.4 litres in 1969, a move that was especially attractive for Ferrari because it meant that the company could use bodywork made more economically from steel without the extra weight costing much in performance. In this form, the 206GT grew up to become one of the marque's greatest classics, the Ferrari Dino 246GT, with the option of fixed-head bodywork or an open, Porsche-style, Targa top.

ENGINE		CHASSIS	
Type	V	Frame	Tubular/alloy sheet construction
No. of cylinders	6		
Bore/stroke mm	86 x 57	Wheelbase mm	2280
Displacement cc	1987	Track – front mm	1425
Valve operation	Twin overhead camshafts	Track – rear mm	1400
		Suspension – front	Independent, wishbones and coil springs
Sparkplugs per cyl.	1		
Compression ratio	9:1		
Induction	3 Weber carburettors	Suspension – rear	Independent, wishbones and coil springs
BHP	180		
Transmission	Five-speed manual gearbox	Brakes	Discs front and rear

PERFORMANCE	
Maximum speed	235 km/h (146 mph)
Fuel consumption	14 litres/100 km (20.2 mpg)

Ferrari 512M

Ferrari 512M

The Ferrari 512 series introduced in December 1969 was intended to be the answer to Porsche's fantastic 917: between them, these two manufacturers took endurance racing into a new dimension. Such complex and expensive cars represented a very ambitious move for these small firms, because at least 25 examples had to be built to qualify them for world championship events as production sports racing cars. The costs of building such exotic machines could only be offset by selling them to suitably wealthy private owners.

Both Ferrari and Porsche had 5-litre 12-cylinder engines which produced so much power that their cars were capable of at least 322 km/h (200 mph), leading to some difficult aerodynamic problems. At first it was thought best to equip the cars with bodywork featuring a tail extended like an aircraft fuselage. Research in wind tunnels had confirmed that a long tail (*coda lunga* in Italian) produced the lowest drag for maximum speed. The trouble was that it made the cars unstable at high speed, with the strong likelihood of their taking off like aircraft. The addition of various trim tabs did little to alleviate the basic problem. As a result, drivers – no matter how brave and experienced – could not use the maximum performance of the cars and had to slow down just to keep the wheels on the ground.

Eventually an English engineer, John Horsman, who was helping run a works Porsche team, solved the problem by cutting off the tail. Although this drastic action reduced the ultimate speed of his projectiles, it was beneficial because the airflow over their rear decks was altered so much that it created downforce. The drivers then found the cars so much more controllable that they could lap faster – despite the reduction in maximum speed.

As demonstrated by Porsche, the advantages were obvious and Enzo Ferrari promptly had the bodywork of the 512S (for Sport) changed for a car called the 512M (*modificato*). These Ferraris then convincingly outran the Porsches!

Motor sport's controlling body never visualized such machines being produced in sufficient quantity to be sold to amateur drivers, so, at the first opportunity, it changed the rules so that engine capacities were limited to 3 litres for the 1972 world championship. Sadly, the 512S and 512M never achieved the success they deserved, chiefly because Ferrari was preoccupied with Formula One and producing prototypes for the revised championship.

ENGINE		CHASSIS	
Type	V	Frame	Monocoque with subframes
No. of cylinders	12		
Bore/stroke mm	87 x 70	Wheelbase mm	2400
Displacement cc	4923	Track – front mm	1518
Valve operation	Twin overhead camshafts	Track – rear mm	1511
		Suspension – front	Independent, wishbones and coil springs
Sparkplugs per cyl.	1		
Compression ratio	11.8 : 1		
Induction	Lucas fuel injection	Suspension – rear	Independent, wishbones and coil springs
BHP	610		
Transmission	Five-speed manual transaxle		
		Brakes	Discs front and rear

PERFORMANCE	
Maximum speed	322 km/h (200 mph)
Fuel consumption	40.4 litres/100 km (7 mpg)

Ferrari 312PB

Ferrari 312PB

Porsche continued to dominate endurance racing with the 917, but retained its predecessor, the smaller 908, for events such as the Targa Florio, where it was more important to be nimble than all-powerful. Ferrari, naturally, produced a similar car, the 312P, towards the end of 1968. This was essentially a scaled-down version of the 612 and 512 cars that ran in the American CanAm series and world championship races. At the same time, Enzo Ferrari was developing a flat-12 cylinder engine for Formula One which could produce more power than the 312P's V12. His enthusiasm reached a new pitch when it was learned late in 1970 that the 1972 world sports car championship would be for 3-litre cars, because it meant that the new prototypes could be developed in parallel with his GP machinery.

The 1971 season was then used to perfect a flat-12 cylinder version of the 312P, the main problem being that the grand prix car on which it was based was far more fragile than the earlier sports racers. The crankshaft, for instance, had only a very limited life at such high power outputs. This new car was called the 312PB (for prototype boxer); the 'boxer' description applied to the flat-12 cylinder engine with its pistons moving backwards and forwards across the car like a prize fighter's fists.

Compared to the big 512 cars, the 312PB was tiny, equipped with simple spyder bodywork like that of the ultra-lightweight Porsche 908/3 which had won the Targa Florio. Initially, the 312PB had headlamps, which were abandoned for races where they were not needed in 1971, then reinstated for the 1972 season with a body modified to meet the latest regulations. These ultimate versions had a wider cockpit and were slightly lower as a result of a season's development.

Six were built so that two fresh cars were always ready to race while the other four were in varying stages of rebuilding. Although they were fragile and only just capable of lasting an average endurance race, this expensive policy ensured that they dominated the world championship in 1972, winning on a combination of sheer speed and reliability. By 1973, however, their rivals, notably Horsman's Mirages and the French Matras, had caught up, and such was the expense of running six 312PBs that they became the last of Ferrari's sports racing cars.

ENGINE		CHASSIS	
Type	Flat	**Frame**	Semi-monocoque with tubular reinforcement
No. of cylinders	12		
Bore/stroke mm	78.5 x 51.5		
Displacement cc	2991	**Wheelbase mm**	2220
Valve operation	Twin overhead camshafts	**Track – front mm**	1425
		Track – rear mm	1400
Sparkplugs per cyl.	1	**Suspension – front**	Independent, wishbones and coil springs
Compression ratio	11.5 : 1		
Induction	Lucas fuel injection		
BHP	440	**Suspension – rear**	Independent, wishbones and coil springs
Transmission	Five-speed manual gearbox		
		Brakes	Discs front and rear

PERFORMANCE	
Maximum speed	322 km/h (200 mph)
Fuel consumption	31.4 litres/100 km (9 mpg)

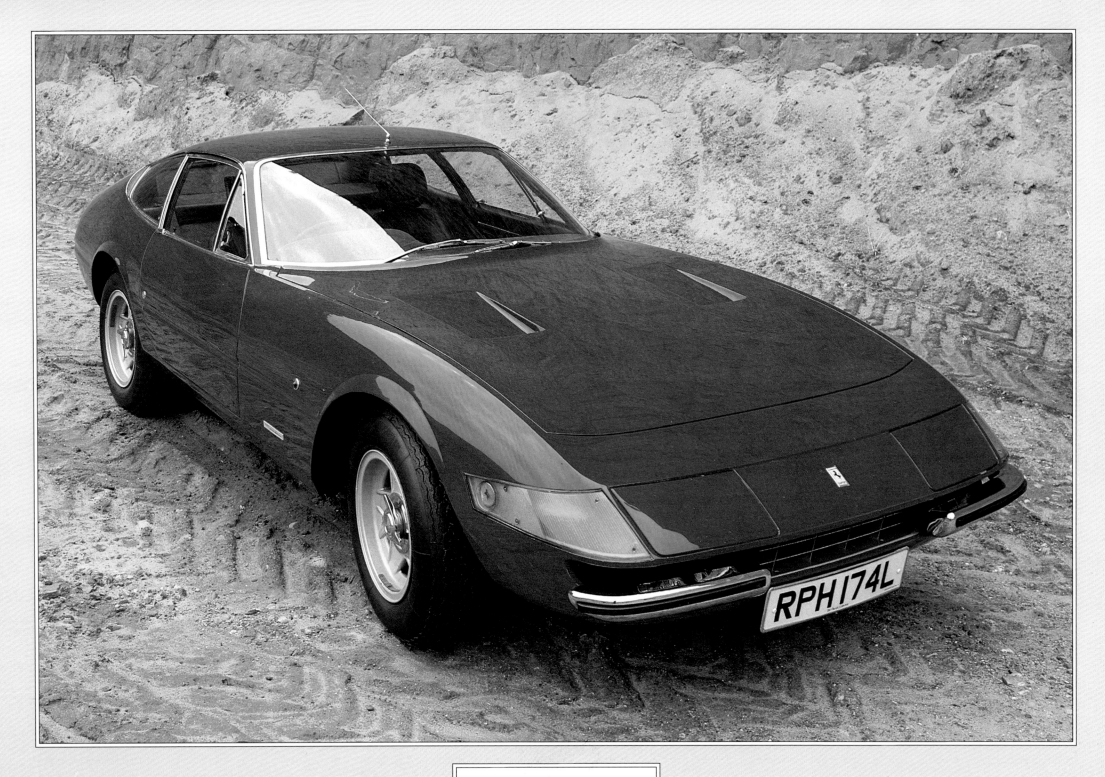

Ferrari 365GTB/4 Daytona

Ferrari Daytona

Almost everybody except Enzo Ferrari called his 365GTB/4 the Daytona in recognition of the marque's exploits on the American track – and Ferrari would have probably have called it the Daytona, too, had he thought of it first! But no matter what the name, it is one of the greatest ever Ferrari grand touring cars, occupying a parallel niche to that of the 250GTO as Ferrari's final expression of what a front-engined two-seater road car should be like.

Enzo Ferrari was keen to ensure that his GT cars did not suffer in performance from the advent of new American exhaust emission regulations in 1968. He therefore had the engine's capacity increased to 4.4 litres like the V12 in his top-line luxury car, the 365GT 2+2, which had replaced the 500 Superfast. In a more highly tuned form for the berlinetta, the Colombo V12 produced 352 bhp on six Weber carburettors – enough to give the Daytona a maximum speed of 280 km/h (174 mph) and to ensure that it would become a legend.

But not only was the Daytona very fast and stable, it was universally recognized as having a very attractive appearance, which had not always been the case with some of its prede-cessors. The bodywork was once again the work of Pininfarina, with the 275GTB/4's rather bulbous wings pared away to a slimmer form and topped off by a delightfully elegant roof. From the practical point of view, the new styling was also a lot better in that it offered far superior visibility through a much increased area of glass. The noseline was also exceptionally neat, with a wide plastic cover for the headlights on European examples, rather like that of the Citroën SM. American cars had to have a different nose, however, to leave the lighting exposed.

The functional new alloy wheels, although of 'five-star' pattern like those used on the Porsche 911, were not in fact inspired by that car – they were of almost identical appearance to those on Ferrari's contemporary GP cars.

A year after the Daytona had been introduced in October 1968, a spyder version was shown and made to special order by Scaglietti. Only a few of these cars were made and it was not until the 365GTB/4 had been superseded that customers started having their berlinettas converted into spyders: with the result that there are now far more open Daytonas around than ever left the factory!

ENGINE		CHASSIS	
Type	V	Frame	Tubular construction
No. of cylinders	12	Wheelbase mm	2400
Bore/stroke mm	81 x 71	Track – front mm	1440
Displacement cc	4390	Track – rear mm	1425
Valve operation	Twin overhead camshafts	Suspension – front	Independent, wishbones and coil springs
Sparkplugs per cyl.	1		
Compression ratio	8.8 : 1	Suspension – rear	Independent, wishbones and coil springs
Induction	6 Weber carburettors		
BHP	352		
Transmission	Five-speed manual gearbox	Brakes	Discs front and rear
		PERFORMANCE	
		Maximum speed	280 km/h (174 mph)
		Fuel consumption	21.5 litres/100 km (13 mpg)

Ferrari 308GTS

Ferrari 308GTS

The Dino 246GT was such a pretty car that it was hard to find anything better to follow it – a task made more difficult by the fact that Ferrari's small car needed to have rear seats if it was to compete with the Porsche 911, Lamborghini Urraco and Maserati Merak. The problem of designing a 2+2 Dino was given to Bertone. The chief snag was finding room for rear seats, no matter how tiny, in a car with its engine where the rear seats ought to be! It was a problem that could only be solved with a relatively long and high roofline to clear the occupants' heads and the transversely mounted engine behind. There was no disguising the fact that so much had to be packed into such a small space: the Ferrari 308GT4 2+2 emerged in 1973 looking nowhere near as attractive as the Dino it replaced, and in addition bearing more than a passing resemblance to its Italian competitors, the Lamborghini and the Maserati.

Despite its extra weight, however, the performance was even better because it had a new twin overhead camshaft 3-litre V8 engine. Its introduction coincided with the world's first oil crisis, though, and there were customers who wanted to appear to be economizing, so Ferrari also produced a 2-litre, small-bore version, the 208GT4 2+2. This was scarcely more economical, in fact, but people could say that it was!

On the other hand, there were a lot of customers who mourned the passing of the 246GT Dino, and even more so its late spyder form, because the 308GT4 was produced only as a fixed-head coupé. Although the 246GT was a fairly heavy car, it was still considered more sporting than the 308GT4 because it had only two seats and looked the part.

Ferrari, therefore, went back to Pininfarina for almost total restyling of the 308 into a new small two-seater Ferrari. The result, the 308GTB, was rather like a larger edition of the 246GT, and sold well because it was so attractive in appearance.

It was an unusual car for Ferrari, however, in that its body was made from corrosion-resistant glass fibre, which had become well established in America with the Chevrolet Corvette. But there were many people who said they could never buy a plastic Ferrari, even in the lovely 308GTS spyder form, so production reverted to steel after just two years in 1976 and 1977.

ENGINE		CHASSIS	
Type	V	**Frame**	Tubular construction
No. of cylinders	8	**Wheelbase mm**	2340
Bore/stroke mm	81 x 71	**Track – front mm**	1460
Displacement cc	2926	**Track – rear mm**	1460
Valve operation	Twin overhead camshafts	**Suspension – front**	Independent, wishbones and coil springs
Sparkplugs per cyl.	1		
Compression ratio	8.8:1	**Suspension – rear**	Independent, wishbones and coil springs
Induction	4 Weber carburettors		
BHP	230		
Transmission	Five-speed manual transaxle	**Brakes**	Discs front and rear
		PERFORMANCE	
		Maximum speed	245 km/h (152 mph)
		Fuel consumption	19 litres/100 km (14.9 mpg)

Ferrari 512BB

Ferrari 512BB

The introduction of Lamborghini's mid-engined Miura in 1966 did not panic Ferrari into following suit immediately, but the popularity of the Dino confirmed that this was the path that would have to be pursued. Using the experience gained from the 250LM, and then from the 206 and 246 Dinos, Ferrari replaced the Daytona in 1973 with the first berlinetta boxer (BB), using what amounted to a flattened version of the Daytona's engine. This 4.4-litre unit was an exceptionally powerful one, making the new 365GT4/BB as fast, if not faster, than Lamborghini's exciting new Countach. The lines of the Boxer followed those of the very successful Dino, although the car was wider and bigger of necessity. The main problem was how to fit such a bulky engine as the flat-12 within a reasonably short wheelbase. Eventually the wheelbase had to be extended to halfway between that of the Daytona and the longer 2+2 GT cars.

Early experiments centred on mounting the flat-12 transversely, as in the Dino, but this proved impractical and eventually it was suspended over the rear axle line, making the Boxer more rear-engined than many other mid-engined cars. The centre of gravity was rather high, too, because the crankshaft was above the wheel centres, but the heavy twin-camshaft cylinder heads were still quite low because it was, after all, a flat engine.

Extensive testing honed the handling to a fine pitch and the 365GT4/BB represented a real advance over the Daytona, even if it lost some of the primitive appeal of 'having the horses at the front'.

By 1976, however, Ferrari was faced with having to update the engine to accord with new pollution and noise regulations, and it was felt that too much performance would be lost by simply detuning the 4.4-litre unit. So the bore and stroke were increased to give an overall capacity of 4.9 litres, which meant that, although the engine was bigger, it produced slightly less power because it could not rev so fast. It gained in torque, however, which made the car easier to drive and the maximum speed of 283 km/h (176 mph) still seemed quite adequate. Reliability was also improved by reverting to the Daytona's dry-sump lubrication, and the rear wheels were widened for better grip. In this form the BB was given the Dino-style 512 designation to emphasize its family links.

ENGINE		CHASSIS	
Type	Flat	**Frame**	Tubular construction
No. of cylinders	12	**Wheelbase mm**	2500
Bore/stroke mm	82 x 78	**Track – front mm**	1500
Displacement cc	4942	**Track – rear mm**	1563
Valve operation	Single overhead camshaft	**Suspension – front**	Independent, wishbones and coil springs
Sparkplugs per cyl.	1		
Compression ratio	9.2 : 1	**Suspension – rear**	Independent, wishbones and coil springs
Induction	4 Weber carburettors		
BHP	340		
Transmission	Five-speed manual transaxle	**Brakes**	Discs front and rear
		PERFORMANCE	
		Maximum speed	283 km/h (176 mph)
		Fuel consumption	21 litres/100 km (13.5 mpg)

Ferrari 400GT

Ferrari 400GT

Ferrari did not abandon the market for large luxury cars when the last 500 Superfast was produced in 1966. The firm phased in the 4-litre 330GTC, which not only had a superior finish to other 300 models, but was bigger and more powerful. Outwardly it had a front like the 500 Superfast and a rear aspect reminiscent of the 330GT; it was one of the best Ferrari all-round road cars ever.

When the time came to change again, in 1968, this car was replaced by a 365GT 2+2, a luxurious 4.4-litre produced in line with the Daytona, but fitted as standard with such creature comforts as air conditioning and power-assisted steering. Experiments were made also with automatic transmission for the first time on a Ferrari, so that potential sales should not be compromised in America, where wealthy customers had often never driven a car with manual transmission. Paradoxically, it was as unthinkable for many Americans to have to operate a gear change and clutch as it was for many Europeans to have to forgo that action, in a Ferrari of all cars!

But it was typical of Ferrari that if automatic transmission was so important to some customers then it would have to be provided and would be the best. To develop and build such a gearbox and torque converter would cost far more than could be recouped, however, especially as only a few people would want it on a Ferrari in any case. So Ferrari simply bought the best – the hydromatic system made by General Motors – for its new top-line luxury car, the 400GT. The decision was made all the more logical because it was also the choice of Rolls-Royce, and of Ferrari's more direct rivals in this sphere, Jaguar.

The new Ferrari, intended to compete with the Jaguar XJ12, was a development of the 365GTC/4 2+2 introduced in 1972 with Pininfarina bodywork that bore a strong resemblance to the Fiat 130 coupé – which was originally meant to be a Lancia! The new Ferrari, however, had more interior space, and for the first time a lot of room for luggage. With this softer image in mind, engine capacity was increased to 4.8 litres, making it much more flexible and far more amenable to being linked with automatic transmission. In both automatic and manual form, the 400GT has had one of the longest lifespans of any Ferrari, selling steadily 10 years after its introduction.

ENGINE		CHASSIS	
Type	V	**Frame**	Tubular construction
No. of cylinders	12	**Wheelbase mm**	2700
Bore/stroke mm	81 x 78	**Track – front mm**	1470
Displacement cc	4823	**Track – rear mm**	1500
Valve operation	Single overhead camshaft	**Suspension – front**	Independent, wishbones and coil springs
Sparkplugs per cyl.	1		
Compression ratio	8.8:1	**Suspension – rear**	Independent, wishbones and coil springs
Induction	4 Weber carburettors		
BHP	325		
Transmission	Automatic or five-speed manual gearbox	**Brakes**	Discs front and rear
		PERFORMANCE	
		Maximum speed	245 km/h (152 mph)
		Fuel consumption	20 litres/100 km (14.1 mpg)

Ferrari Testa Rossa

Ferrari Testa Rossa

In 1984, Ferrari did what many people had thought impossible: launched a new car that was faster, more exciting and more refined than the Boxer – and fittingly called it the Testa Rossa after the company's most emotive sports car of the past, reserving the name GTO for a competition 308.

The engine of the new Testa Rossa followed the *quattrovalvole* (4 valves per cylinder) theme established in later versions of the 308 and a 2+2 Mondial. In this fuel-injected 48-valve form, the 4.9-litre boxer engine was rated at 390 bhp.

The Boxer's bodywork was substantially revised in aluminium to pare down the weight, with great attention paid to reducing the frontal area for better aerodynamics. In pursuit of this theme, side-mounted radiators were used rather than one in the nose, with distinctive slatted air intakes of a type that had first appeared on the Mondial. The most prominent change, however, apart from a continuation of the slatted theme around the nose and tail, was a substantial increase in width.

The widened track had the effect of noticeably reducing the body roll that had been inherent in having a high centre of gravity. The opportunity was taken at the same time to change to tyres of extremely low profile (45 series Michelins) now that the suspension settings could be revised to retain sufficient ground clearance and the wheel arches reshaped. The visual effect of using such tiny tyres was offset by a prominent waistline. The overall effect was to make the new Testa Rossa look squatter and more purposeful than the Boxer, and at the same time the handling and maximum speed were improved.

The four valve per cylinder layout not only increased the power output, but in conjunction with Bosch fuel injection made the new car more economical, with the added advantage of having more torque distributed over a wide band.

From the driver's point of view, apart from the benefits to handling and performance, it was also possible to see far more for the glass area was increased as the wing line was slimmed down. And from the passenger's point of view there was now far more room for luggage without a massive water radiator in the nose. Although the Testa Rossa was still essentially a Boxer, Ferrari worked a magical transformation in these superb refinements.

ENGINE		CHASSIS	
Type	Flat	**Frame**	Tubular construction
No. of cylinders	12	**Wheelbase mm**	2500
Bore/stroke mm	82 x 78	**Track – front mm**	1976
Displacement cc	4942	**Track – rear mm**	1976
Valve operation	Single overhead camshaft	**Suspension – front**	Independent, wishbones and coil springs
Sparkplugs per cyl.	1		
Compression ratio	9.2:1	**Suspension – rear**	Independent, wishbones and coil springs
Induction	Bosch fuel injection		
BHP	390		
Transmission	Five-speed manual transaxle	**Brakes**	Discs front and rear
		PERFORMANCE	
		Maximum speed	291 kh/h (181 mph)
		Fuel consumption	20.2 litres/100 km (14 mpg)